# Women, Wealth & Real Estate

Danielle Pierce

*Disclaimer: None of the information taken in this book should be taken as financial and/or legal advice. Please be sure to consult with a trusted financial or legal professional as deemed necessary*

## Dedication

This book is dedicated to my mother, first and foremost. She played the hell out of the hand she was dealt and I am eternally grateful for all the lessons that you provided. I also dedicate this book to my babies Noelani, Serena, Mujahid and Makayla. May you all have the ongoing courage and resiliency to create bold, purposeful and passionate lives. I love you to infinity and beyond.

# Introduction

I was born and raised in the south suburbs of Chicago. My immediate family was poor and so was all of my extended family. My mother had aspirations of going to college on a full scholarship. Unfortunately, she wasn't able to accomplish this task due to becoming pregnant in high school. Aside from that, there were 4 other children that followed in quick succession. As is the case with many of African descent in this country; my father was not in the background.

Given my background, it's a minor miracle that I was able to attend college, with a full tuition scholarship no less! I also graduated on time with a Bachelor of Science in Accountancy from one of the top schools in the Midwest! This book was written for parents and children that have dreams of being successful, but are not sure which path to walk.

I wrote this book to present options outside of the SAD "standard American dream."
I wrote this book to provide a roadmap to financial success outside of an increasingly expensive college degree.

I wrote this book to speak to the younger generation and let them know that, yes, there are paths to success besides doing what their parents did. The millennial generation gets a bad rap most of the time. Yet, as a whole, Generation X and Y are doing a tremendous job of breaking barriers, forging their own paths, asking all the right questions and generally creating the life of their dreams.

What could be better than CREATING the life you desire as opposed to taking what's handed to you?

Let's begin.

# Table of Contents

# Chapter 1:
# The Beginning

## My Earliest Memory-

It sounds remarkably shocking when I say this out loud to other people OR write it down. My earliest memory on this earth is my Dad barging through the patio door and attacking my mom. I remember this event so clearly as it's one that seems to be permanently seared in my memory. After my dad started hitting my mother, I ran into the closet and just started screaming and screaming at the top of my lungs. I didn't stop until my older sister came into the room to give me a hug and help me to calm down. I remember the police knocking on the door and my sister opened the door to let them in. I distinctly remember looking around and saw my dad still standing there, breathing hard. My mother, who has worn wigs for as long as I can remember, stood there as well looking ashamed, afraid and with her wig askew on her head.

To this day, my mother and I have never spoken a single word about **ANY** of those incidents.

> **It wasn't until many years later that I would realize just how much I learned and absorbed with my first row seat to the domestic violence that plagued my childhood home.**

When I was 10 years old, I made a vow to myself to read 100 books over summer break. At that time, I loved Hardy Boys, Babysitter's Club and Nancy Drew books. I could read a book in less than a day. At that time, I would literally read for HOURS on end.  My mother had hundreds of books in our household when I was a child and she fostered my love of reading.

I believe I started to read initially as a way to get closer to my mother and to earn her approval. But, I eventually got to a point where my love for reading became completely genuine.

Looking back, it is quite clear to me that reading kept me out of a lot of trouble. I've never been the child with dozens of friends at any point. I've always had a tight circle of just a handful of friends and that trend has continued to this day.

Unfortunately, reading didn't keep me out of trouble 100% of the time. Right around 6th grade, I had decided that I was "bored" with school and that I didn't need to attend on a regular basis. So, for the remainder of that year, I ditched school two or three times a week until I had racked up over 28 absences in 1 semester.

In my super cool 13 year old brain, I figured as long as I kept calling the school (while pretending to be my mom, of course) that my absences would be excused and no one would be any wiser. After all, I told myself, the work was super easy and I could still get at least all B's even without going to class.
This continued all the way up until that fateful day when I called the office again, pretending to be my mom and she just so happened to be standing RIGHT IN THE OFFICE while I was on the phone.

Man.......

I got home from school that day and received the shock of a lifetime! I have never BEFORE or SINCE witnessed my mom get so mad at me before. She would later recall to me that she could only "see red" and that she really had to restrain herself while talking to me. I am certain I made the situation worse with my flippant, nonchalant attitude. I recall telling her that it "wasn't a big deal" because the work was boring, the teachers didn't care and I still got better grades than any of her "other children" anyway.

Too bad my ability to assess dangerous situations wasn't on par with my smart mouth! My mother pushed me so hard I fell into a wall AND put a huge hole in it. As I look back at this incident, I believe both of us were in shock. My mother had NEVER laid a hand on me before and I believe my mom was in shock because I had always been a follower of the rules and the child she could rely upon to remain on point.

Needless to say, I never cut school after that. It was still as boring and uninspiring as ever, but I didn't like to see my mother that upset and so I vowed to never be the cause for her to feel that way again.

I transitioned into high school at the ripe old age of 13. I really didn't know what to expect or how to act. Thirteen really is a very awkward age and so I masked all that awkwardness with the most annoying KNOW IT ALL attitude EVA! At that point in my life, not a single person could tell me anything about anything ESPECIALLY my mom. I am quite sure that my mom wanted to sucker punch me at least once a week based solely on my poor attitude. In reality, I was just insecure, lacking in confidence and also dealing with sexual molestation by my sister's boyfriend.

The molestation started when I was 12 and he was 19 years old. I had always had a crush on my sister's boyfriend. My father wasn't around and he was the only adult male that seemed to show a genuine interest in my life and my brother's lives. He seemed to really like being around us, telling stories, playing games and taking us places – especially me. He used to call me his "little sister" and that made me feel so proud and happy. Based on what I know now, I realized that what he was doing was setting the stage for what was to come. I now know that child molesters are often highly skilled manipulators and excel at getting their victims to know, like and trust them. Oddly enough, it wasn't until I was 37 years old that I recognized that experience as being outside of my control. For years, I had made the assumption that I was a willing participant and that I was old enough and smart enough to know right from wrong.

That traumatic experience didn't completely stop until I was 16 years old. I was finally able to end that relationship by starting up another one with a boy who lived across the street from me. That relationship was a train wreck from the beginning and I KNEW it. The only reason that relationship began was to have an excuse to no longer deal with my sister's boyfriend. The guy across the street was every mom's nightmare for their daughter. On top of all of that, he wasn't even that bright intellectually. We would have conversations and he would urge me to "speak English" in this disdainful tone of voice and frequently accuse me of talking down to him. I can remember thinking to myself, "Danielle, what the FUCK are you doing with your life?" That relationship was highly verbally abusive and a few times physically abusive. It ended for good my freshman year in college after he started threatening my life (again) and stalking me. I realized that I was punishing myself for the relationship with my sister's boyfriend and I had taken enough punishment.

During college I found my groove sophomore year and I was an above average student. Attending a school like University of Illinois allowed me the flexibility to not attend class, study on my own and still get good grades. (See, Mom, I knew what I was doing all along!)

## Introduction to Real Estate

My interest in real estate started in my 2nd year at the University of Illinois. I was looking for an apartment and I kept seeing the name Gabe's Place Apartments. I was fascinated with this Gabe and wanted to know if this was one person or a company or what? I ended up leasing an apartment from Gabe and then I set out on a mission to meet Gabe in person. I sent a few emails to the leasing office asking to meet with him personally to discuss how he got started in real estate. Eventually, he responded and invited me to his estate in Urbana. Gabe turned out to be very arrogant, pompous and very prideful BUT I believe he had earned the right to be. Gabe told me that he came to this country at 19 with no money. He didn't have a car and rode his bike everywhere. He told me that he worked multiple jobs, didn't go out and saved all his money. In fact, he worked and saved until he had reached $63,000 for a down payment for his first 6 unit building. And the rest, as they say, is history. He went on to own multiple apartment buildings and became wealthy in the process. Gabe took the time to give me my first insight into being a real estate mogul and for that, I am eternally grateful.

## Corporate Life

Like many people within my age group, my entire definition of success was centered around college education, graduation and then subsequent employment in a corporate position. Of course, with hard work, dedication and loyalty to my employer – I would inevitably break all glass ceilings and eventually make partner in a top 5 public accounting firm.

Well, my journey kinda didn't go that route! The primary reason that it didn't is because I REALLY disliked corporate America. I found the work to be immeasurably boring and unfulfilling and I was literally yawning and fighting off sleep every single day. Looking back, I have to realize that it was complete and utter madness. How does it make sense for someone still in her 20s to be so desperately unhappy and bored every.single.day? What's worse is that this was considered completely normal – everyone was in the same boat. During lunch, or coffee breaks and sometimes after hours, everyone would just bitch and moan about how they hated their jobs and/or their managers. I literally saw all of this within the first 90 days and I KNEW that I was not going to be able to go down this path indefinitely. I stuck around at this job about 3 years and then I transitioned into internal audit which was a different (read: equally boring) area of accounting.

There's a funny thing about human nature. Many of us live our entire lives in search of "something different" because we refuse to honor our instincts and our innate sense of balance. This was the case with my transition out of public accounting into internal audit. I discredited what my mind and body was telling me and overrode that in favor of this great new job – which somehow was supposed to be the answer to all my problems. As you can probably guess, I was equally unfulfilled in that role.

I remember, like it was yesterday, the day that rumors started circulating that our company was about to be acquired in a takeover attempt and all positions within the department were going to be eliminated. I remember the excitement and surge of joy at losing my audit position. Around that same time, I had attended a workshop in the Chicagoland area hosted by Guy Williams and I decided that I was going to become a real estate broker. As it turned out, I received my real estate license in 2006, started my first flip in 2007 and was laid off in 2007 as well. I took my lay-off as a sign that I was heading in the right direction and that I was destined to be an entrepreneur. I completed my first flip and received a check for $26,908.57 and I was literally over the damn moon! I thought I was rich and didn't need to work for a while. In my head, I thought this real estate thing is super easy and I could totally get used to this lifestyle. As it turns out, I was definitely in over my head and had spoken a little too soon.

**Life After Corporate**
I want to take this time to reveal some of the darkest moments I experienced in those early years after being laid off. While it was definitely true that I wanted out of corporate, the reality is that I didn't have a plan for myself outside of working in corporate America. I had been conditioned from childhood to live that lifestyle and when the universe gave me what I asked for, I was just blowing in the wind. I didn't have a plan, a blueprint or ANYTHING which would help me start my life as an entrepreneur. Looking back, I should have been a lot more frightened than I was. I reckon that's one of the beautiful parts about your 20s. You can find yourself in extreme danger and you are just too dumb to know it lol!

I spent the better part of 2 years just kicking it, going to concerts, not punching a clock and spending all the money I had received when I left corporate and spending all the money from my very first flip.

I didn't invest it.
I didn't even buy additional properties.
I didn't pay off debt.
I didn't even pay off my student loan debt.
I didn't save any money either.
Now, you might have forgotten by now, but I will go ahead and remind you that I did graduate from one of the top accounting programs in the country with a 3.2 GPA. So, for sure, the topic of finances was not brand new for me. I had taken economics, statistics, advanced accounting and advanced finance classes. Since that was the case – what explains all the poor financial decisions I have made over the years?

Well, there are a few reasons for those financial mishaps and I'll delve into each of them, one by one.

# #1 - Lack of Vision

I had never truly envisioned myself in the role of entrepreneur and thus I didn't connect any of what I was learning in college to my real life. I performed well in those jobs because I was expected to and I didn't want to appear incompetent. It simply didn't occur to me to transfer those skills over to my real life and my real business. I believe I thought my fledgling business wasn't good enough or worthy enough to have operational systems and procedures in place. I don't want you to read this and conclude that I am anti-college as that is far from the truth. I am definitely against going to college without a solid plan of building networks and resources AFTER college. At the time, I looked at college as a separate experience from the rest of my life instead of the foundational building block for the rest of my life.

## #2 - Lack of Support

Every single person within my immediate and extended family worked in a traditional job setting. At that time, within my circle of friends everyone worked a job, specifically a corporate 9 to 5 job. So, 100% of the people that I talked to, hung out with and socialized with in any capacity –were NOT entrepreneurs.

Social conditioning is a very real and prevalent phenomenon. Under these conditions, it is exceedingly difficult for the seed of entrepreneurship to ever plant itself. Certainly, if the seed is planted, then nurturing it is just simply out of the question.

There is a very good reason for the saying: "change your circle and change your life." Unfortunately, I didn't fully embrace this philosophy at that time either. My version of being your own boss meant doing what you wanted when you wanted, waking up when you wanted, not punching a clock and passing out a few business cards here and there.

It was SUCH a train wreck and my thinking was absolutely detrimental to my success as a business owner. When I think about where these notions came from, I think I just made them all up! Honestly, where else would they have come from since I didn't consistently interact with a single entrepreneur for the first 2 years I called myself one?

## #3 – Laziness

I am a firm believer in calling a spade a spade and I know for sure that I was very lazy in those early days. I seemed to be under the delusion that success would come my way because I "deserved it," I was highly intelligent and because I spoke a few affirmations over my life here and there. I would never have admitted it then, but I think I also believed I would be successful because I was pretty!

Lord! The utter foolishness –

What I now know is that success is a function of positive affirmation, hitting macro sized goals on a consistent basis, laser focus and the biggest thing: doing what you need to do even when you don't feel like it. During those early years, I didn't spend a whole lot of time on DOING! I was too busy reading, writing, making vision boards, passing out business cards and generally just making a whole lot of plans and doing nothing about it. I have pages and pages of notes from those years and I realized very few of those poorly laid plans.

To be honest, I have gone back and forth with myself as to whether I was truly lazy or just plain didn't know what to do. The best answer is that it's likely a combination of both.

## The Shift

If all of what I have written previously describes you, you may now be wondering when the "big shift" will occur. You want to know what is the defining event or scenario that will ignite that small flame of entrepreneurship you have burning inside of you. To be perfectly honest, I don't believe there is a one size fits all answer to this question. My big shift came out of sheer desperation. I have tracked my income every month since 2007 and there was one month in particular which I will never forget. It was June 2009 and my income for that entire month was $348 IN TOTAL. Granted, I didn't have any children yet to take care of, but that month became a turning point in my life. I initially started with a whole lot of negative self-talk, rounded out with healthy doses of anger, frustration and regret.

Based on my experience, many people that begin entrepreneurial endeavors after leaving corporate feel compelled to talk about the experience as if it's this perfectly magical endeavor without hiccups. There continues to be this odd sort of competition between corporate employees and entrepreneurs. Each side is constantly trying to prove how great their life is and how horrible the other person's life is.

I definitely felt compelled to lie about how my experience was going, given how badly I had talked about my corporate experience. I didn't want to look foolish, silly or admit that I had made a mistake. I for sure, didn't want to admit that I didn't know what the hell I was doing OR even why I was doing it.

So, in true control freak fashion, I gave the impression that I knew exactly what I was doing and that I was making money hand over fist!

In reality, I was floundering on a daily basis and just couldn't seem to get a handle on what I was supposed to do on a daily basis. Looking back, none of this is actually very surprising, considering my upbringing. Everyone I know worked a job. Everyone I knew was paid on a Friday and broke again within a few short days. Everyone I knew ALWAYS made comments like: "that has to wait until I get paid" or "I don't have the money."

So, I did what any fledgling and struggling entrepreneur would do in this situation – I went fleeing back to my safety and comfort zone of corporate America.

I interviewed at a few places but the oddest thing happened... I was NOT able to get hired at any of the places where I applied. Up until that point, I had always interviewed well and obtained job offers with ease. I was having the opposite experience this time around. I simply couldn't get hired.

So, I was at a very uncomfortable and unfamiliar place in life. I had no money. I had no clue how to go about the business of being an entrepreneur. And I couldn't run back to my comfort zone of corporate America because I was being rejected for every available opportunity.
The turning point came when I decided to start having children. Any woman that has been pregnant can likely relate to the sense of wonder, hopefulness, joy and just plain ole delight (and fear) that comes with being charged with bringing a whole human into the world.

## Working With Your Spouse
In the very beginning of my career as a property preservation vendor – I worked with my husband. But, if I'm completely honest – it was a train wreck from the very beginning. Also, the phrase "worked with" is misleading as well. Essentially, I dragged him along into my vision of the business. I had the initial idea, I took all the necessary steps to complete the applications, I did all follow up and I laid the groundwork. I spent a lot of time convincing him about the merits of the business as well.

The business relationship was tumultuous largely because our personal relationship was the same. Also, our personalities are very different and our operational methods didn't align either. And then there was the fact that I had been self-employed since 2007 and my husband had never been self-employed.

As many of us know now or will eventually come to realize, the mindset of an employee is far different than the mindset of an entrepreneur. Entrepreneurship requires a strong desire to execute AND real life execution. If a person is "trying," "in the process of" or "working on" whatever IT is, that just simply means that they aren't actually doing any of those things. If I had approached the situation logically for even a second, I would quickly have surmised that a business partnership with my husband would not be suitable. But, of course, I did not and that is why I'm urging anyone reading these pages to NOT make the mistakes that I did. If your goal is to select a partner for your business, you have to bring the person into the partnership based on the traits and characteristics that the person currently has. You have to identify their top strengths and weaknesses. You really have to assess if your respective work styles are complementary. In short, the person should bring qualities to the table that complement AND supplement your skill set. If you base the decision solely on the assumption that because you are married you will work well together, you will likely fail.

# Chapter 2:
# Tax Lien Investing

If I had to select the single best method to get started investing in real estate, tax lien investing emerges as the absolute best choice.

Tax lien investing refers to the purchase and acquisition of tax lien certificates. Most typically, tax lien investing takes place during the annual or bi-annual tax sale. You may also see the following language utilized as well: commissioner sale, sheriff's sale, deed sale or scavenger sale. Each of these terms has slightly different meanings and you should have a full understanding of each term PRIOR to investing. For now, just be aware that any or all of these types of sales presents an opportunity for a buyer to purchase properties at substantially discounted pricing and without the hassles of bank financing.

Tax lien investing is going to be ideal for the individual that has saved at least several thousand dollars and has credit issues and/or just doesn't want to obtain bank financing.

**Important Points To Remember:**

- ➢ Purchases must be paid for by close of business on the DAY of purchase.
- ➢ Typically, only cash is accepted or certified funds. Personal checks and credit cards are not allowed.
- ➢ Financing is not an option. If you don't pay the winning bid amount by close of business, you risk being assessed a penalty fee, forfeiting the property AND being banned from future tax sales
- ➢ Research is going to be absolutely critical to your success as a tax lien investor
- ➢ In most cases, you won't be responsible for the

additional back taxes outside of your winning bid. To clarify, if total back taxes owed is $10,000, and your winning bid is $3,000 – you will NOT be responsible for the remaining $7,000. You will be responsible for future tax bills.

**Frequently Asked Questions:**

*How much money do I need to invest in tax liens?*
This answer depends upon where you decide to invest. As previously mentioned, $2,500 might be a great start for a place like Lake County Indiana. It may not even cover the registration fee for Los Angeles

*Are all registration fees $500? What happens to the fee if you don't purchase any tax liens?*
The registration fee will vary based on the city, state and county where you decide to invest. In many cases, the registration fee will act as a credit to any bids you win and will be returned if you don't make any purchases. HOWEVER, this can and likely will vary around the country. For example, in Cook County Illinois, the registration fee is $1,000

*What is the difference between a tax lien sale and a tax deed sale?*

A tax lien sale is the purchase of a certificate which is essentially an interest in the property. Purchasing a tax lien DOES NOT mean that you are the owner of a property...yet. There are multiple steps that have to be followed in order to officially obtain the tax deed to the property. These steps are the domain of your attorney which is why you MUST have one on your team. If you attend a tax deed sale and purchase a tax deed, then you have just purchased the property. There are STILL other steps to follow and you should STILL retain an attorney under these circumstances as well.

*You mentioned that I would have to pay current year taxes as well – how much will those be?*

I know this is starting to sound like a broken record BUT the property tax amount is location dependent. If you have done your due diligence, you will have a very good idea of how much property taxes are for the neighborhood you have selected.

*Do I need an attorney? Can't I just do all the work myself?*

No, you don't NEED an attorney and it's certainly possible to do the work yourself. But, it is my blanket recommendation to hire an attorney if you are brand new to tax lien investing. Once you gain experience, you can then decide to opt out of using an attorney if you feel comfortable with the steps. I know experienced investors that don't use an attorney to cut costs and I know experienced investors who prefer to pay an attorney so they can devote more time to locating properties.

*What is the name of the attorney you utilized during the Lake County Tax Sale?*
Jeffrey A. Piposar, Esq.
412.527.1548
Jeff@jeffreypiposar.com

*I don't want to actually own any properties – I just want to utilize tax lien investing as an investment strategy – is this possible?*

Yes, tax lien investing has become a popular investment strategy as it can offer double digit returns with very low risk. The goal is to purchase liens on those properties where you anticipate the owner will likely redeem your tax certificate. There is both an art and a science component to this particular investment strategy. For example, during your research you may find an expensive property where the owner had some temporary difficulties and fell behind $5,000 in taxes. You might drive by the property and note that it's very well maintained and still owner occupied. You may then decide to purchase this lien with the idea that the owner will eventually come up with the money to pay the back taxes. Under this scenario, you could likely receive the initial $5,000 investment back, plus any attorney's fees that you incurred during the process along with the statutory interest for that particular county which can be anywhere from 5 to 25%!

*How long is the redemption period?*

This also varies based upon location. Do keep in mind that the redemption period can be changed by the local government as well. For example, the redemption period might ordinarily be 2 years, but local officials may elect to have a sale where redemption is only 6 months. This is why it's critical to complete YOUR own research. Relying on preliminary Google searches and listening to people tell you about what they've "heard" is a sure way to miss out on tax lien investing opportunities.

*How do I determine how much repairs a property will need prior to purchasing?*
Determining repair costs is both an art and a science as well. After all, you are not usually able to access the interior of any of the properties prior to buying the tax lien. Your repair estimate is solely based on an external review if the property is occupied. Now, if the property is vacant, you may be able to get a little more creative by looking into windows etc. But, still you have to keep in mind that you have NO AUTHORITY to enter these properties prior to purchasing the tax lien OR after. Your authority will begin once you have an order for deed that is signed by the judge.

*OK, I have followed all the steps and now I am officially the owner of several properties. What now? Do I rent or flip the properties?*

Congratulations. Hopefully, during the research phase you identified an exit strategy prior to investing. Your exit strategy is contingent upon your cash/credit on hand and your real estate investment goals along with current market conditions. If properties are located in a down market, you may opt to renovate and rent the units until market conditions improve. If the market is a hot one with many recent sales, you may opt to renovate the property and place it on the market immediately. Another option you may have is to do a minimal rehab and attempt to wholesale the property. Research. Research. Research.

*I want to invest in an area with a $500 minimum starting bid. When is the next tax sale for Lake County Indiana?*
The next sale will likely be in March 2018 – As of the time of this writing, specific dates aren't yet available.

*I need additional help with this process. I am afraid to begin on my own.*
Please review the resources in the Appendix section and schedule a consult with me at **www.daniellepierce.com**

## Quick Start Guide

➢ Contact your local assessor's office to inquire about the next tax sale for the county you'd like to invest. Ask about any registration fees and also find out the deadline to register. Be sure to ask the timeframe for the redemption period.

➢ Make sure to have at least $2,500 dollars on hand for purchases. Please do keep in mind that this amount can vary substantially depending upon location. For example, $2,500 won't take you very far in places like Los Angeles.

- ➢ Download the list of properties if available online or obtain it from the assessor's office.
- ➢ Do make sure to consult with experienced tax lien investors prior to attending the sale. This can be done by simply joining local investment groups on Facebook or Meetup.com
- ➢ Don't bombard experienced investors with every single question you have.
- ➢ Do complete your independent research and make a short list of questions to ask the experienced party. Independent research means physically going to see the properties. You should also buy a few local papers to get a feel for what's happening in the neighborhood. Talk to some neighbors and business owners. It's not really possible to do too much in this regard, so explore all options available to you.
- ➢ Don't ever bid sight unseen unless you have psychic abilities or the desire to lose money
- ➢ Do offer to ask how you can best assist the experienced party to compensate them for their time
- ➢ Do hire an attorney experienced in tax lien investors.
- ➢ It's a great idea to also pay additional tax bills that are issued during the redemption period to protect your investment.
- ➢ Do attend local government meetings to ask about upcoming developments to determine up and coming areas to invest.

# A Snapshot Into My Experience As A Tax Lien Investor

Sale Date: March14th-17<sup>th</sup> 2017, Lake County
Indiana
Winning Certificates As Follows:
$500.00
$500.000
$1,200.00
$800.00
**Total Initial Investment: $3,000**

Registration Fee: $500.00
Amount Due In Cash On The Last Day Of The Sale: $2,500
($3k less registration fee)
Redemption Period: 120 Days
Properties Redeemed By Owner: 1

Note: If a property is redeemed, the tax lien investor receives back whatever money they paid for the tax lien along with 10% interest AND any attorney's fees that were paid.

Attorney's Fees: $600 Per Winning Bid – Total Cost: $2,400

Total Acquisition Costs For 4 Properties:
$5,400 ($3,000 + $2,400)

Based on this example, it is clear that it's possible to acquire properties really cheaply at the tax lien auction. For more information on how to get started, please feel free to schedule a consult with me at www.daniellepierce.com

# Chapter 3: Property Preservation

Many people, when they think of real estate careers, generally think of working as a traditional buyer or seller agent. In fact, there are actually dozens of different, highly profitable niches within the real estate industry. Some of these careers are listed below:

> Wholesaler
> Property Flipper
> Bird Dogger
> Tax Lien Investor
> Appraiser
> Home Inspector
> Property Preservation Contractor

Another option is to complete broker price opinions (BPOs) on a full time basis. Broker price opinions are valuation reports that are utilized by banks and servicing companies in the case of deed in lieu, loan modification and/or refinance. BPO reports are less detailed than full blown appraisals. Banks hire brokers to complete BPO's so that they don't have to pay an appraiser several hundred dollars more.

In this chapter, we are going to focus exclusively on the property preservation industry. Property preservation is essentially the repair and maintenance of bank owned or managed properties. There are a handful of companies that service properties on a national basis. The 2nd tier is what I like to call regional firms which are companies that don't cover the entire country but service multiple states. Aside from the regional contractors, there are local companies that continue to emerge on an almost monthly basis. I will provide more detail about each of these categories shortly.

The absolute best thing about the property preservation industry is the fact that it offers a really high revenue and income potential. Once a preservation vendor develops a knowledgeable team and obtains a contract with the right company, the revenue potential is easily millions of dollars. However, as we will discover shortly, there is a lot that goes into partnering with the right company and establishing a team.

Other benefits to the preservation industry include time flexibility, absence of micromanagement and the ability to establish and operate your company in the manner which you, as the owner, deem to be most suitable.

There are several disadvantages which are detailed below:

1. Industry is largely unregulated. There is no certification or license required to be a property preservation vendor
2. It can be difficult to obtain a contract with a national company and establish a large enough territory to bring in significant revenues
3. Locating and retaining subcontractors is an ongoing challenging process for most primary vendors
4. It can be difficult to manage dozens of work assignments each month, disperse to the appropriate subcontractors and oversee each work assignment to ensure appropriate completion.
5. There are many preservation companies (usually the smaller local companies) that routinely bring on new subcontractors and either do not pay at all OR their vendor pricing is so low that nearly all the

profit margin is removed.

**Frequently Asked Questions:**

*How much money do I need to get started?*

You need at least $3k at a bare minimum if you seriously thinking about getting started. This only holds true if you plan to set your business up to completely outsource everything. If your intent is to complete all of the work in house, your start up costs could easily be $25,000 or more. The reason for the dramatic increase is simple – you will need to purchase materials, supplies and equipment in order to complete the assigned work items. There is a possibility of renting all of the necessary equipment for the first few months, until you are in a position to buy. Renting eats into your profit margin pretty significantly and you really have to make a thorough assessment before undertaking this alternative.

*What types of insurance do I need?*

You will absolutely need general liability and professional liability (also called Errors and Omissions). Some companies require you to obtain workman's compensation insurance as well.

*My state has an exemption for worker's compensation insurance – do I still need to obtain worker's compensation insurance?*

The answer to this depends upon the specific preservation company. Some states, like Illinois and Texas, for example do NOT require worker's compensation insurance if you are a business owner AND you don't have any employees. In other words, everyone that works with your company is considered a 1099 independent contractor. If you live in a state that allows this type of exemption, then most companies will waive the worker's compensation insurance requirement. As of the time of this writing, Safeguard is the only company I am aware of which STILL requires worker's compensation insurance even if you live in a state with an exemption.

*Where should I obtain my insurance and how much should it cost?*
The best place to obtain insurance is from an insurance broker. Insurance brokers have the ability to provide quotes from multiple lenders. You have to specifically indicate that you need a company that covers property preservation activities. Several companies do NOT cover property preservation activities at all. Hiscox is an example of a company that doesn't provide coverage for property preservation companies. There is no real standard but I would expect to pay at least $2k for the entire year for a combined general liability and errors and omissions policy. Workman's comp varies tremendously in coverage. In Illinois, there are places that offer coverage for the year for around $1,200. Texas, on the other hand, offers workman's comp starting at $2k+ per year. I can't stress the importance of shopping around in this regard. I would obtain at least 4 quotes before making a final decision.

*How much money will I make?*

Of course, there are no absolute guarantees on income. However, the very first step is to make sure that you obtain a contract as a primary vendor with a national company. If you decide to do anything less than this option, your income potential is automatically reduced. Once you are well established with a national company you should hit at least $100k in revenue within the first 12 months. You have to remember that $100K in revenue is on the very low end of the spectrum for a full time established vendor in this industry. The other thing to keep in mind is that the only purpose to achieving high revenue is to maximize your net profit. If your revenue is $200k, and your expenses are $175k, that's not a very profitable enterprise, is it? Set your profit goals upfront, pay yourself first, and keep an eagle eye on those expenses. To learn more about the process of paying yourself first, I recommend reading Profit First by Michael Makalowiecz.

*What's the best way to find good subcontractors?*

As I mentioned previously, locating and keeping good subs is literally the life blood of your business...and it's also the most challenging aspect. If you spend some time talking to any vendor, you will quickly find out that the struggle to keep good contractors is a challenge that EVERYONE repeatedly faces. Of course, placing ads on online through sites like Craigslist and Indeed are helpful.    But, I think the majority of vendors become complacent after they find a few good candidates. Once those contractors leave the company, then they are back to searching for more replacements. I believe that you have to ALWAYS BE RECRUITING in this industry if you ever hope to build a business that is long term and operates independent of you as the owner.   Your online ads should be renewed and reposted every single week indefinitely. You can never have too many good contractors.

*All of the preservation companies I have reached out to either haven't responded or they don't need any more vendors in the area due to oversaturation. What should I do?*

In this situation, my first recommendation is to continue to reach out to the preservation companies via email or a call once every 2-3 weeks going forward. You will quickly find out that this industry is ever changing and there are often periods of high turnover. When I was just getting started with my company in Illinois with Altisource it was very slow for the first 5 months or so. Then, one of the vendors lost their territory due to performance issues. Just like that, we went from receiving a few work orders per week to 300 per month! This allowed our company to reach over $300k in revenue in 2014 which was the first full year of operations. If you keep reaching out, there WILL absolutely come a time when a new vendor is needed and if you are correctly positioned, that new vendor could be you. The other recommendation I have is to ask the preservation company which cities and states they require coverage. At one point, I was completing work assignments in 12 states (I have since scaled back to only those states which generate the most revenue). You can certainly provide services in other states if you desire. However, please keep in mind that you will need to have a solid system, operational guidelines, hiring guidelines and the funds to cover your higher payroll costs. You may also be required to obtain a business license in other states as well if you begin to receive a significant portion of your revenue from out of state.

**Quick Start Guide**
- ➢ Do research each company before submitting an application to join their vendor network
- ➢ Do submit applications only for the national preservation companies. Your ultimate goal is to

obtain a contract as a primary vendor with a national preservation company

➢ Do work with someone that has experience obtaining preservation contracts before submitting your application. Preservation companies are looking for specific criteria and requirements in their vendors

➢ Do ensure that your time management, money management and organizational skills are stellar. While it is difficult to obtain a contract as a primary vendor, it is pretty easy to lose a contract. Contracts are pulled for any or all of the following reasons: late work orders, incomplete work orders, improper conduct from subcontractors in the field, poor quality documentation and poor communication. Almost all of the aforementioned reasons stem from poor organization and time management skills.

➢ Do ensure to have appropriate systems in place prior to obtaining a contract. You will need a system for tracking hours worked for yourself and your team, a system to keep track of subcontractor documentation, a system to manage multiple work orders from different companies and a system to manage any inventory, equipment and supplies. Finally, you will need a system to keep track of all administrative paperwork regarding insurance, licensing and/or any required bonds

➢ Don't hire subcontractors solely based upon the fact that they are your family and/or close friends.

➢ Don't partner with someone that has never

operated a business before. The mindset of an employee is worlds apart from that of an entrepreneur.

➢ Don't partner with someone solely because you are in a relationship with them and/or they are your best friend. Choose your partner as objectively as possible. Evaluate your partner as you would evaluate anyone interviewing for the position. The right partner can absolutely make or break your company. Choose wisely.

➢ Do contact an insurance broker to obtain general liability, professional liability and worker's compensation insurance. Please note that some states, such as Illinois, do not require you to obtain worker's compensation insurance unless you have actual employees (vs 1099 contractors). With that being stated, some preservation companies will allow you to obtain a waiver from worker's comp insurance. Other companies will require you to obtain worker's compensation insurance irrespective of the state in which you reside.

➢ Do make sure to save between $3k-$5k prior to obtaining a contract.

➢ Do make sure to raise your personal credit score and business credit score, if possible prior to applying to become a vendor.

If you would like a more detailed explanation into getting a property preservation contract, please click here to access the online learning platform: http://www.women-wealth-real-estate.thinkific.com/

# Chapter Four:
# Start Your Business
# in 30 Days

For the last 2 years, it seems that entrepreneurship has become THE thing to do. There is no shortage of individuals and companies urging everyone to "become their own boss" and "create financial freedom." Many of these people look down upon those with a 9 to 5 as still being "on the plantation" or taking part in "corporate slavery."

As with most things, the truth is 1) whatever holds true for you and 2) typically somewhere in the middle of both extremes.

I can tell you one truth, though, just the act of starting a business is not a ticket to financial freedom...and you can quote me on that one, honey!

Yes, I am a huge believer and advocate of the entrepreneur lifestyle. I am an even greater advocate for establishing a solid foundation upon which to build. With that being stated, my preferred method of business start-up is to being a sole proprietorship.
Sole proprietorships are super easy, super quick and can generally be set up for less than $100 and will take just over 30 days.

For those of you not familiar, a sole proprietorship is a business that is NOT considered a separate entity from the owner. In short, you as the business owner can be personally held liable in the event that someone sues your business – because YOU are the business.

Now, if you are like most people, you might have read that and completely freaked out. You may have even headed on over to legal zoom to research how to start a corporation. My personal opinion is that IF you have the funds available, it makes perfect sense to start your business as a C-corporation or S-corporation.

But, if you are like many of the people I have encountered over the years, and you are unsure what you want to do, have very limited funds and/or limited expertise, then a sole proprietorship might be perfect for you.

And, keep in mind, that transitioning from a sole proprietorship to a corporation is usually only a matter of paying a CPA or attorney a few hundred dollars to set it up on your behalf. It can be accomplished in a matter of days.

As always, make sure to consult with your financial professional prior to taking any of the actions mentioned above. I had to learn the value the hard way of having a good financial professional on my team. Don't repeat my mistake, ok?

## Quick Start Guide
  ➢ Do select a name for your business and select a

domain name as well in order to build your website. There is typically an online database to search to make sure the name you want is available. You can purchase your domain name from www.godaddy.com

➢ Select your social media handle and set up profiles on Facebook, LinkedIn and Instagram at a minimum. Be sure to visit www.namchk.com to determine which handles are available. Ideally, you want all social media handles to be the same for brand consistency.

➢ Do complete your business registration on the Secretary of State's website. You will need a business address in order to complete the process. Many people set up their business using their home address, which I don't typically advise my clients to do. If someone searches for your business at some point, they will now discover where you live as well. I usually tell my clients to set up a virtual business address which can be done at a place like www.regus.com

➢ Do request a DUNS number via www.dandb.com

➢ Do set up a dedicated phone line for your business – this can even be done using a Google Voice number.

➢ Do create a basic 4 page site using either Wix or Wordpress.

➢ Do set up an account with Google G-Suites so you can establish a professional email address.

➢ Do create a 20 second commercial about your business so you have a ready answer to the question: "what does your business do?"

# Chapter 5: Business Credit

The benefits of business credit are significant in a variety of ways. Perhaps, the clearest benefit is that it allows business owners the ability to purchase supplies, equipment and/or fund payroll without dipping into any personal funds. Another widely touted benefit is that business credit reports separately from your personal credit report, in most cases.

There are plenty of myths and alternative facts surrounding business credit so I wanted to take this time to dispel some of the popular ones.

**Myth #1**
Personal credit is not considered when applying for business credit.

Response:
This is likely the biggest myth with regard to business credit. I have spoken to multiple business credit experts and the consensus is the same: personal credit is a factor when applying for business credit. In fact, for the average small business owner, personal credit is likely the largest single deciding factor in whether an individual obtains business credit and the amount of business credit they receive.

**Myth #2**
Business credit is difficult to obtain

Response:

Business credit is not difficult to obtain. There are several key requirements which are outlined later in the chapter.

## Q & A with PK Patel of Midwest Credit Corporation

*Question: Is it possible to obtain business credit without providing a personal guarantee?*
Answer: As of now, it is only possible to obtain "vendor lines" without providing a personal guarantee, PROVIDED the company also has a Dunn & Bradstreet profile already established. Examples of vendor lines include Home Depot, Lowes etc (Think store credit cards which are only able to be used at that particular store)

*Question: What minimum personal credit score is necessary to build business credit the fastest?*
Answer: At a minimum, the person should have a 700 middle credit score to be eligible.

*Question: Is it possible to obtain business credit a business that was just created 30 days ago?*
Answer: Absolutely. Of course, the dollar amount may not be as high. However, if the other criterions are met, then start up businesses can receive business credit.

*Question: Since a personal guarantee is required, does that mean that my business credit lines will report to my personal credit reports?*
Answer: This varies depending upon the type of business credit you receive. If you specifically ask to only be considered for business credit lines that DO NOT report to the personal credit bureaus, that request will be honored.

*Question: When applying for business credit, how many inquiries should I expect on my credit report?*

Answer: You should certainly be aware that applying for business credit will most likely result in multiple hard pulls on your personal credit reports. However, as the end consumer, you should always make your expectations known if you prefer to limit the number of inquiries. A knowledgeable lender will only direct you to those credit lines where you will be most likely approved and thus limit the number of total inquiries. There can be as many as 8 hard pulls on each credit report individually (total of 24) or 8 pulls for a specific credit report.

*Question: Does it make sense to establish a banking relationship prior to applying for credit?*

Answer: Within the last 2 to 3 years, banking relationship has started to weigh into the lender's business credit underwriting process. There are at least several banks in the Chicagoland area where the absence of a banking relationship automatically reduces eligibility by 25%.

*Question: Which personal credit score is utilized when applying for business credit?*

Answer: This answer will also vary depending upon the lending institution that is utilized. In years past, FICO was the gold standard and enjoyed an overwhelming market share. As of now, there are a couple of dozen versions of FICO alone. Each credit bureau has its own score AND individual banks have come up with their own in house scoring models as well! When applying for business credit, be sure to ask as many questions as possible to determine which scoring model will be used.

*Question: What is the single most effective tip I can follow to increase my scores rapidly?*

Answer: If a person can lower their credit utilization to 10% or less, that will have the most dramatic impact on scores. High credit score achievers, in general, don't carry high revolving debt balances. Think of it this way, if a person is willing to carry debt at double digit interest rates, that person is either not financially savvy or is headed towards financial trouble.

## Quickstart Guide

➤ Do make sure to have at least a 680 middle personal credit score

➤ Do make sure to establish an actual business structure. Sole proprietorships are perfectly acceptable as long as they are properly established and registered

➤ Do make sure that your company has been registered for at least one year. It is possible to obtain business credit for startup companies. In cases like this, the personal credit score becomes even MORE critical.

➤ Do make sure to obtain a DUNS number. If your business has been registered for at least 6 months, a DUNS number has likely been generated and you just need to locate it. For brand new businesses, you can request a DUNS number within about 30 days of business registration. Obtain a DUNS number here: www.danb.com

➤ Do make sure to work with a reputable company to establish business credit. A quick search of "business credit" will yield thousands of thousands of search results of companies all promising to help your company establish business credit. If you are completely unfamiliar with obtaining business credit, the sheer amount of options will be extremely overwhelming. I'd recommend researching each company you are interested in, selecting no more than 5 at a time to interview, check Google and Yelp reviews and work with a local company if at all possible where you can personally meet the company representatives.

## Appendix – Resources

For help with setting up a business as a repair/property preservation vendor, please visit http://www.women-wealth-real-estate.thinkific.com/

**Tax Liens:**

George Howard, Financial Freedom University, www.myffu.com

**Business Credit Assistance:**

Midwest Corporate Credit

www.midwestcorporatecredit.com, 630-376-6063

Real Estate Investing via Crowdfunding

Adina McCollough, visit Buy Back The Block LLC on Facebook

**Personal Credit Assistance:**

MNH Financial Services,

http://mnhfinancialservices.com/

Made in the USA
Las Vegas, NV
24 May 2021